Copyrigh

© Chef Leonardo 2021
of this book may be reproduced without prior permission of the author.

No part of this document may be reproduced, duplicated or transmitted in any way in digital or printed form. The distribution of this publication is strictly prohibited and any use of this document is not permitted without the prior written consent of the publisher. All rights reserved.

It is guaranteed the accuracy and integrity of the information contained in this document, but no kind of responsibility is assumed. It is the sole and absolute responsibility of the intended reader, in terms of misinterpretation of the information through carelessness or the use or misuse of any policies, processes or instructions contained within the book. Under no circumstances may the publisher be prosecuted or blamed for any damage done or monetary loss incurred as a result of information contained in this book, either directly or indirectly.

The rights are owned by the respective authors and not by the publisher.

Legal notice: This book is protected by copyright. It is for personal use only. You may not modify, distribute, sell, use, quote or paraphrase any part of the contents of this book without the specific consent of the author or owner of the copyright.

In accordance with the law.

Disclaimer:

Please note that the contents of this book are for educational and entertainment purposes only.

Table of content

Chapter 1. Ground Beef 4

1. Meat Loaf 4
2. Beef Chorizo 7
3. Ground Beef and Bell Peppers 10
4. Cabbage and Beef Fry.................... 13
5. Light Beef Enchiladas 16
6. Italian Meatballs........................... 20
7. Healthy Avocado Beef Patties.......... 23
8. Crazy Japanese Potato and Beef Croquettes 26
9. Cool Cabbage Fried Beef 30
10. Beef Soup 33
11. Beef Skillet.................................. 36
12. Sloppy Joe................................... 40
13. Turmeric Meatloaf......................... 44
14. Beef Casserole 48
15. Light Shepherd Pie........................ 52
16. Stuffed Tomatoes 56
17. Cheesy Beef and Broccoli 60
18. Mini BBQ Meatloaf......................... 64
19. Beef and Spaghetti Squash Casserole 68

Recipes

20. Taco Cabbage Casserole 72
21. Butter Beef and Spinach 75
22. Asian Salad 79
23. Ground Beef and Green Beans and Tomatoes 83
24. The Surprising No "Noodle" Lasagna . 87
25. Sloppiest Sloppy Joe 91
26. Bacon Cheeseburger 95

Chapter 1. Ground Beef

1. Meat Loaf

Preparation Time: 5 minutes

Cooking Time: 5-6 hours

Servings: 6

Ingredients

- 2-pound lean ground beef
- 2 whole eggs, beaten
- ¾ cup milk
- ¾ cup breadcrumbs
- ½ cup chicken broth (see recipe)

- ¼ cup onion, finely diced
- 3 garlic cloves, minced
- 1 teaspoon low-sodium salt
- ¼ teaspoon freshly ground black pepper
- ¼ cup low sodium chili sauce
- Nonstick spray

Directions:

1. Mix the beaten eggs, milk, oatmeal, spices, onion, garlic, and chicken broth until well combined.
2. Mix in the beef and place in a 5-quart or larger slow cooker, sprayed with non-stick spray.
3. Cover and cook on low for 5 to 6 hours.
4. Serve with low-sodium ketchup.

Nutrition: Calories 280, fat 10g, carbs 9g, protein 37g, Fibre 1g, potassium 648mg, sodium 325mg

Recipes

Note:

2. Beef Chorizo

Preparation Time: 10 minutes

Cooking Time: 10 minutes

Servings: 4

Ingredients:

- 3 garlic cloves, minced
- 1 lb. 90% lean ground beef
- 2 tbsp hot chili powder
- 2 tsp red or cayenne pepper
- 1 tsp black pepper
- 1 tsp ground oregano
- 2 tsp white vinegar

Directions:

1. Mix all ingredients together in a bowl thoroughly then spread the mixture in a baking pan.

2. Bake the meat for 10 minutes at 325 degrees F in an oven.

3. Slice and serve in crumbles.

Nutrition: Calories 72. Protein 8 g. Carbohydrates 1 g. Fat 4 g. Cholesterol 25 mg. Sodium 46 mg. Potassium 174 mg. Phosphorus 79 mg. Calcium 14 mg. Fibre 0.8 g.

Recipes

Note:

3. Ground Beef and Bell Peppers

Recipes

Preparation Time: 10 minutes

Cooking Time: 10 minutes

Serving: 3

Ingredients:

- 1 onion, chopped
- 2 tablespoons coconut oil
- 1 pound ground beef
- 1 red bell pepper, diced
- 2 cups spinach, chopped
- 1/8 teaspoon salt and pepper to taste

Directions:

1. Take a skillet and place it over medium heat
2. Add onion and cook until slightly browned
3. Add spinach and ground beef
4. Stir fry until done
5. Take the mixture and fill up the bell peppers
6. Serve and enjoy!

Nutrition: Calories: 350 Fat: 23g Carbohydrates: 4g Protein: 28g

Recipes

Note:

4. Cabbage and Beef Fry

Preparation Time: 5 minutes

Cooking Time: 15 minutes

Serving: 4

Ingredients:

- 1 pound beef, ground
- ½ pound bacon
- 1 onion
- 1 garlic clove, minced

- ½ head cabbage
- 1/8 teaspoon salt and pepper to taste

Directions:

1. Take a skillet and place it over medium heat

2. Add chopped bacon, beef and onion until slightly browned

3. Transfer to a bowl and keep it covered

4. Add minced garlic and cabbage to the skillet and cook until slightly browned

5. Return the ground beef mixture to the skillet and simmer for 3-5 minutes over low heat

6. Serve and enjoy!

Nutrition: Calories: 360 Fat: 22g Net Carbohydrates: 5g Protein: 34g

Recipes

Note:

5. Light Beef Enchiladas

Preparation Time: 8 minutes

Cooking Time: 15 minutes

Serving: 6

Ingredients

- 1-pound (around 650 grams) ground lean beef
- ½ cup shallots, chopped
- 1 clove of garlic
- 1 tsp of ground cumin
- ½ tsp cayenne pepper
- 1 can or small (200-gram jar) of enchilada sauce
- 12 corn tortillas
- 1/8 teaspoon extra cheese on top (optional)
- 1/8 teaspoon kosher pepper

Directions:

1. In a medium frying pan with 1 tsp of oil, brown the ground beef and the shallots (around 5-6 minutes).

2. Add the garlic and spices and toss to mix well. Cook until meat will become brown, and shallots will be soft and transparent. Add half of the enchilada sauce toss and cook for another 5 minutes.

3. Lightly toast the corn tortillas for 30-40 seconds on the toaster.

4. Distribute in each the remaining enchilada sauce and the ground beef mixture. Wrap and roll from one side to another to make enchiladas.

5. Sprinkle optionally a bit of grated cheddar cheese on top and place in the microwave for 1-2 minutes to melt the cheese and serve.

Nutrition 286 Calories 26.3g Protein 201mg Sodium 224mg Potassium 146mg Phosphorus

Recipes

Note:

6. Italian Meatballs

Preparation Time: 7 minutes

Cooking Time: 18 minutes

Serving: 12

Ingredients

- 1/2 pounds of ground beef chuck,
- 2 eggs, beaten
- ½ cup of red onion, chopped
- ½ cup of rolled oat flakes
- ½ tsp of garlic salt

- 1 tsp of dried oregano
- 3 tbsp of parmesan cheese
- 1 tbsp of tomato paste
- ½ tsp of black pepper

Directions:

1. Preheat your oven at 375 F/190C.

2. Mix all the ingredients.

3. Shape into small balls (around 1 inch) and place on a Pyrex or baking sheet.

4. Bake for 16 minutes

5. Remove from the oven and serve with a light tomato sauce or hot sauce and rice.

Nutrition 133 Calories 5.8g Carbohydrate 62.7mg Sodium 252mg Potassium 166mg Phosphorus

Recipes

Note:

7. Healthy Avocado Beef Patties

Preparation Time: 15 minutes

Cooking Time: 10 minutes

Serving: 2

Ingredients:

- 1 pound 85% lean ground beef
- 1 small avocado, pitted and peeled
- 1/8 teaspoon fresh ground black pepper as needed

Directions:

1. Pre-heat and prepare your broiler to high.

Recipes

2. Divide beef into two equal-sized patties.

3. Season the patties with pepper accordingly.

4. Broil the patties for five minutes per side.

5. Transfer the patties to a platter.

6. Slice avocado into strips and place them on top of the patties.

7. Serve and enjoy!

Nutrition: Calories: 568 Fat: 43g Net Carbohydrates: 9g Protein: 38g

Recipes

Note:

8. Crazy Japanese Potato and Beef Croquettes

Preparation Time: 10 minutes

Cooking Time: 20 minutes

Serving: 10

Ingredients:

- 3 medium russet potatoes, peeled and chopped
- 1 tablespoon almond butter
- 1 tablespoon vegetable oil

Recipes

- 3 onions, diced
- ¾ pound ground beef
- 4 teaspoons light coconut aminos
- 1 cup all-purpose flour for coating
- 2 eggs, beaten
- 1 cup panko breadcrumbs for coating
- ½ cup oil, frying

Directions:

1. Take a saucepan and place it over medium-high heat; add potatoes and sunflower seeds water, boil for 16 minutes.

2. Remove water and put potatoes in another bowl, add almond butter and mash the potatoes.

3. Take a frying pan and place it over medium heat, add 1 tablespoon oil and let it heat up.

4. Add onions and fry until tender.

5. Add coconut aminos to beef to onions.

6. Keep frying until beef is browned.

7. Mix the meat with the potatoes evenly.

8. Take another frying pan and place it over medium heat; add half a cup of oil.

9. Form croquettes using the potato mixture and coat them with flour, then eggs and eventually breadcrumbs.

10. Fry patties until golden on all sides.

11. Enjoy!

Nutrition: Calories: 239 Fat: 4g Carbohydrates: 20g Protein: 10g

Recipes

Note:

9. Cool Cabbage Fried Beef

Recipes

Preparation Time: 5 minutes

Cooking Time: 15 minutes

Serving: 4

Ingredients:

- 1-pound beef, ground and lean
- ½ pound bacon
- 1 onion
- 1 garlic clove, minced
- ½ head cabbage
- 1/8 teaspoon pepper to taste

Directions:

1. Take skillet and place it over medium heat.
2. Add chopped bacon, beef, and onion until slightly browned.
3. Transfer to a bowl and keep it covered.
4. Add minced garlic and cabbage to the skillet and cook until slightly browned.
5. Return the bottom beef mix to the skillet and simmer for 3-5 minutes over low heat.
6. Serve and enjoy!

Nutrition: Calories: 360 Fat: 22g Net Carbohydrates: 5g Protein: 34g

Recipes

Note:

10.   Beef Soup

Preparation Time: 10 minutes

Cooking Time: 40 minutes

Serving: 4

Ingredients:

- 1-pound ground beef, lean
- 1 cup mixed vegetables, frozen
- 1 yellow onion, chopped
- 6 cups vegetable broth
- 1 cup low-fat cream Pepper to taste

Directions:

1. Take a stockpot and add all the ingredients the except cream, salt, and black pepper.

2. bring back a boil.

3. Reduce heat to simmer.

4. Cook for 40 minutes.

5. Once cooked, warm the cream.

6. Then add once the soup is cooked.

7. Blend the soup till smooth by using an immersion blender.

8. Season with salt and black pepper.

9. Serve and enjoy!

Nutrition: Calories: 270 Fat: 14g Carbohydrates: 6g Protein: 29g

Recipes

Note:

11. Beef Skillet

Preparation Time: 10 minutes

Cooking Time: 30 minutes

Servings: 3

Ingredients

- 1 cup lean lean ground beef
- 1 cup bell pepper, sliced
- 2 tomatoes, chopped
- 1 chili pepper, chopped
- 1 tablespoon olive oil
- ½ cup of water

Directions:

1. Heat up olive oil in the skillet and add lean ground beef.

2. Roast it for 10 minutes.

3. Then stir the meat well and add chili pepper and bell pepper. Roast the ingredients for 10 minutes more.

4. Add tomatoes and water.

5. Close the lid and simmer the meal for 10 minutes.

Nutrition: 167 calories, 16.1g protein, 6.3g carbohydrates, 8.8g fat, 1.6g Fibre, 46mg cholesterol, 50mg sodium, 508mg potassium.

Recipes

Note:

12. Sloppy Joe

Recipes

Preparation Time: 10 minutes

Cooking Time: 35 minutes

Servings: 4

Ingredients:

- 1 cup lean ground beef
- 1 cup onion, diced
- ½ cup sweet peppers, diced
- 1 teaspoon minced garlic
- 1 tablespoon canola oil
- 1 teaspoon liquid honey
- ½ cup tomato puree
- 1 teaspoon tomato paste

Directions:

1. Mix up canola oil and lean ground beef in the saucepan.

2. Add onion and sweet pepper and stir the ingredient well.

3. Cook them for 10 minutes.

4. Then add honey, tomato puree, and tomato paste. Mix up the mixture well.

5. Close the lid and cook it for 25 minutes on medium heat.

Nutrition: 134 calories, 7.6g protein, 8.7g carbohydrates, 7.7g fat, 1.9g Fibre, 22mg cholesterol, 34mg sodium, 170mg potassium.

Recipes

Note:

13. Turmeric Meatloaf

Preparation Time: 15 minutes

Cooking Time: 50 minutes

Servings: 6

Ingredients:

- 1 teaspoon ground turmeric
- 1 teaspoon chili flakes
- 2 oz minced onion
- 2 cups lean ground beef
- 2 tablespoons semolina
- 1 tablespoon ketchup
- 1 egg, beaten
- 1 teaspoon olive oil

Directions:

1. Brush the meatloaf mold with olive oil.

2. Then in the mixing bowl, mix up all ingredients from the list above.

3. Transfer the meat mixture in the prepared meatloaf and flatten it well.

4. Bake the meatloaf at 375F for 50 minutes.

5. Then cool it well and slice into servings.

Nutrition: 136 calories,16.5g protein, 4.4g carbohydrates, 5.5g fat, 0.4g Fibre, 73mg cholesterol, 82mg sodium, 285mg potassium.

Recipes

Note:

14. Beef Casserole

Servings: 5

Preparation Time: 15 minutes

Cooking Time: 45 minutes

Ingredients:

- 1 cup zucchini, grated
- 1 teaspoon margarine
- 8 oz lean ground beef
- 1 bell pepper, chopped
- 1 cup tomatoes, crushed
- 1 teaspoon dried thyme
- 1 teaspoon ground black pepper
- 4 oz low-fat feta, crumbled

Directions:

1. Grease the casserole mold with margarine.

2. Mix up ground black pepper, dried thyme, and lean ground beef together.

3. Put the mixture in the casserole mold and flatten well.

4. Top it with zucchini, bell pepper, and crumbled low-fat feta.

5. Add crushed tomatoes and cover with foil.

6. Bake the beef casserole in the preheated to 385F oven for 45 minutes.

Nutrition: 164 calories,18.9g protein, 5.6g carbohydrates, 8g fat, 1.6g fibre, 8mg cholesterol, 56mg sodium, 379mg potassium.

Recipes

Note:

15. Light Shepherd Pie

Preparation Time: 15 minutes

Cooking Time: 40 minutes

Servings: 4

Ingredients:

- 1 cup lean ground beef
- 1 teaspoon tomato paste
- 1 teaspoon chili powder
- ½ cup green peas
- 1 cup potatoes, mashed
- ¼ cup low-fat yogurt
- 1 teaspoon olive oil

Directions:

1. Put lean ground beef in the skillet.
2. Add olive oil and chili powder.
3. Roast the meat for 10 minutes.
4. Then add tomato paste and mix it up.
5. After this, transfer the mixture in the casserole mold.
6. Top it with green peas and mashed potatoes.
7. Flatten the potato well.
8. Then sprinkle it with yogurt and cover with foil.

9. Bake the shepherd pie for 30 minutes at 375F.

Nutrition: 139 calories, 13.9g protein, 10.2g carbohydrates, 4.5g fat, 2.1g fibre, 35mg cholesterol, 54mg sodium, 435mg potassium.

Recipes

Note:

16. Stuffed Tomatoes

Recipes

Preparation Time: 20 minutes

Cooking Time: 35 minutes

Servings: 2

Ingredients

- 4 oz lean ground beef
- 2 tablespoons low-fat yogurt
- 1 teaspoon dried thyme
- ½ teaspoon chili powder
- 2 tomatoes
- ¼ cup of water

Directions:

1. Cut the tops of tomatoes and scoop the tomato meat from them
2. Then mix up lean ground beef, thyme, and chili powder.
3. Fill the prepared tomatoes with meat mixture.
4. Then top them with yogurt and put in the casserole mold.
5. Add water and cover them with foil.
6. Bake the tomatoes for 35 minutes at 375F.

Nutrition: 142 calories,19.3g protein, 6.5g carbohydrates, 4.1g fat, 1.9g fibre, 52mg cholesterol, 62mg sodium, 573mg potassium.

Recipes

Note:

17. Cheesy Beef and Broccoli

Preparation Time: 5 minutes

Cooking Time: 10 minutes

Servings: 4

Ingredients

- 85% lean ground beef – 1 pound
- Salt – 1 tsp.
- Garlic powder – ½ tsp.
- Dried parsley – ½ tsp.
- Dried oregano – ¼ tsp.
- Butter – 2 Tbsp
- Beef broth – ¾ cup
- Broccoli florets – 2 cups
- Heavy cream – ¼ cup
- Shredded cheddar cheese – 1 cup

Directions:s:

1. Brown the beef on Sauté in the Instant pot.
2. Press Cancel and sprinkle seasonings over meat.
3. Add broccoli, broth, and butter. Close the lid.
4. Press Manual and cook for 2 minutes on High.
5. When done, press Cancel and stir in cheddar and heavy cream.
6. Serve.

Nutrition: Calories: 476 Fat: 33.5g Carb: 3g Protein: 29.9g

Recipes

Note:

18. Mini BBQ Meatloaf

Preparation Time: 5 minutes

Cooking Time: 25 minutes

Servings: 4

Ingredients

- 85% lean ground beef – 1 pound
- Onion – ½, diced
- Green pepper – ½, diced
- Almond flour – ¼ cup
- Shredded mozzarella cheese – ¼ cup
- Egg - 1
- Salt – 1 tsp.
- Pepper – ¼ tsp.
- Garlic powder – 1 tsp.
- No sugar added barbecue sauce – ¼ cup

Directions:

1. Except for the barbecue sauce, mix all ingredients in a bowl.

2. Make two loaves and place into loaf pans.

3. Pour sauce on top and cover with foil.

4. Pour 1 cup water into the Instant pot and place the steam rack.

5. Place the meatloaf pans on steam rack.
6. Close the lid and press Manual.
7. Cook 25 minutes on High.
8. Serve.

Nutrition: Calories: 340 Fat: 20.3g Carb: 4.2g Protein: 26.4g

Recipes

Note:

19. Beef and Spaghetti Squash Casserole

Preparation Time: 10 minutes

Cooking Time: 20 minutes

Servings: 4

Ingredients

- Spaghetti squash – 6 pounds, cooked and scraped out into long strands with a fork
- No sugar added tomato sauce – 1 cup
- Whole-milk ricotta – ½ cup
- Grated parmesan cheese – ¼ cup
- Butter – 3 tbsps
- Dried parsley – ½ tsp.
- Garlic powder – ½ tsp.
- Dried basil – ¼ tsp.
- Salt – ½ tsp.
- Pepper – ¼ tsp.
- 85% lean ground beef – 1 pound, cooked
- Shredded mozzarella cheese – 1 cup, divided
- Water – 1 cup

Directions:
1. Place the squash into a bowl.

2. Add remaining ingredients except for water (reserve ½ mozzarella).

3. Mix and pour mixture into a bowl.

4. Sprinkle remaining cheese on top and cover with a foil.

5. Pour water into the Instant pot and place steam rack.

6. Place bowl on the steam rack and close the lid.

7. Press Manual and cook for 10 minutes.

8. Do a natural release.

9. You can broil the dish in the oven for a few minutes to brown the top.

10. Serve.

Nutrition: Calories: 628 Fat: 37.5g Carb: 9g Protein: 36.5g

Recipes

Note:

20. Taco Cabbage Casserole

Preparation Time: 5 minutes

Cooking Time: 4 minutes

Servings: 4

Ingredients

- 85% Lean ground beef – 1 pound
- Shredded white cabbage – 2 cups
- Salsa – 1 cup
- Salt – 1 tsp.
- Chili powder – 1 Tbsp
- Cumin – ½ tsp.
- Water – ½ cup
- Shredded cheddar cheese – 1 cup

Directions:

1. Brown the beef on Sauté in the instant pot.

2. Then add remaining ingredients, except for cheese.

3. Close the lid and press Manual.

4. Cook 4 minutes on High.

5. Do a quick release and stir in cheddar.

6. Serve.

Nutrition: Calories: 393 Fat: 23g Carb: 5.1g Protein: 29.5g

Recipes

Note:

21.   Butter Beef and Spinach

Preparation Time: 2 minutes

Cooking Time: 10 minutes

Servings: 4

Ingredients

- 85% lean ground beef – 1 pound
- Water – 1 cup
- Fresh spinach – 4 cups
- Salt – ¾ tsp.
- Butter – ¼ cup
- Pepper – ¼ tsp.
- Garlic powder – ¼ tsp.

Directions:

1. Brown the beef on Sauté in the Instant pot.

2. Remove into a bowl. Drain grease and clean the pot.

3. Add water into the pot and place steam rack.

4. Place the bowl with the beef on top.

5. Add garlic powder, pepper, butter, salt, and spinach.

6. Cover with a foil and close the lid.

7. Press Manual and cook 2 minutes on High.

8. Do a quick release.

9. Remove foil, stir, and serve.

Nutrition: Calories: 272 Fat: 19.1g Carb: 0.6g Protein: 18.3g

Recipes

Note:

22. Asian Salad

Recipes

Prep Time: 10 minutes

Cook Time: 15 minutes

Servings: 4

Ingredients

- Ground beef – 1 pound
- Coconut aminos – 2 Tbsp
- Garlic – 2 cloves [minced].
- Sesame seed oil – 2 Tbsp
- Apple cider vinegar – 1 tsp.
- Sesame seeds – 1 tsp.
- Green onion – 1 [chopped].

Directions:

1. Heat sesame seed oil in a pan over medium heat.
2. Add garlic and brown for 1 minute.
3. Add beef. Stir-fry for 10 minutes.
4. Make coleslaw mixture, add it into a pan and toss to coat. Cook for 1 minute.
5. Add salt, pepper, coconut aminos, Sriracha, and vinegar. Stir-fry for 4 minutes.
6. Add sesame seeds, and green onions, toss to coat.
7. Serve.

Recipes

Nutrition: Calories: 281 Fat: 14.3g Carb: 1.5g Protein: 34.7g

Recipes

Note:

23. Ground Beef and Green Beans and Tomatoes

Recipes

Preparation Time: 15 minutes

Cooking Time: 30 minutes

Servings: 6

Ingredients

- 1 teaspoon of olive oil
- 1 pound of lean ground beef
- 1 chopped medium onion
- 1 tablespoon of minced garlic
- 1 teaspoon of dried thyme
- 1 teaspoon of dried oregano
- ½ a pound of green beans, ends trimmed and cut up into 1-inch pieces
- 2 can of petite diced tomatoes with juice
- 2 cans of beef broth
- ½ teaspoon flavored vinegar and pepper as needed
- Freshly grated parmesan for serving

Directions:

1. Set your pot to Sauté mode and add oil, allow the oil to heat up

2. Add ground beef and stir well as it cooks

3. Once the beef is browned up, add chopped onion, dried thyme, minced garlic, dried oregano and cook for 3 minutes

4. Add petite-dice tomatoes alongside the juice and beef broth

5. Allow them to heat for a while

6. Trim the beans on both ends and cut into 1-inch pieces

7. Add beans to your pot

8. Lock up the lid and cook on SOUP mode for 30 minutes

9. Perform a quick release

10. Season with flavored vinegar and pepper

11. Serve freshly with a grating of parmesan

12. Enjoy!

Nutrition: Calories: 327 Fat: 24g Carbohydrates: 12g Protein: 19g

Recipes

Note:

24. The Surprising No "Noodle" Lasagna

Preparation Time: 10 minutes

Cooking Time: 10 minutes

Servings: 8

Ingredients

- 1 pound of ground beef
- 2 cloves of minced garlic
- 1 small sized onion
- 1 and a ½ cups of ricotta cheese
- ½ a cup of parmesan cheese
- 1 large sized egg
- 25 ounces of marinara sauce
- 8 ounces of sliced mozzarella

Directions:

1. Set your pot to sauté mode and add garlic, onion, and ground beef

2. Take a small bowl and add ricotta and parmesan with egg and mix

3. Drain the grease and transfer the beef to a 1 and a ½ quart soufflé dish

4. Add marinara sauce to the browned meat and reserve half

5. Top the remaining meat sauce with half of your mozzarella cheese

6. Spread half of the ricotta cheese over the mozzarella layer

7. Top with the remaining meat sauce

8. Add a final layer of mozzarella cheese on top

9. Spread any remaining ricotta cheese mix over the mozzarella

10. Carefully add this mixture to your Soufflé Dish (with meat)

11. Pour 1 cup of water to your pot

12. Place it over a trivet

13. Lock up the lid and cook on HIGH pressure for 10 minutes

14. Release the pressure naturally over 10 minutes

15. Serve and enjoy!

Nutrition: Calories: 607, Fat: 23g, Carbohydrates: 65g, Protein: 33g

Recipes

Note:

25.   Sloppiest Sloppy Joe

Recipes

Preparation Time: 10 minutes

Cooking Time: 15 minutes

Servings: 4

Ingredients

- ½ a cup of white quinoa
- 2 tablespoon of olive oil
- 1 large sized chopped up yellow onion
- 1 large sized Italian frying pepper completely stemmed, chopped up and deseeded
- 2 pound of lean ground beef
- 2 teaspoons of minced up garlic
- 1 piece of 18 ounce can have crushed tomatoes
- ½ cup of old-fashioned oat tolls
- ¼ cup of packed dark brown sugar
- 2 tablespoon of Dijon mustard
- 2 tablespoon of Worcestershire sauce
- 2 tablespoon of apple vinegar
- 2 tablespoons of paprika
- ¼ teaspoon of ground clove

Directions:

1. Open your instant pot and add in the grains

2. Pour in as much water, as required to cover up the grains

3. Lock up the lid and let it cook at high pressure for 3 minutes

4. Quick release the pressure

5. Open and drain out the quinoa in a fine mesh sieve set in your sink

6. Heat up your cooker in sauté mode and pour some oil

7. Add in the pepper, onion and cook for 4 minutes

8. Then, add in the crumbled ground beef and garlic and keep stirring them nicely

9. Let it cook for 6 minutes until the beef is not pink anymore

10. Then, stir in the tomatoes, brown sugar, oats, mustard, vinegar, cloves, paprika and Worcestershire sauce alongside the nicely drained quinoa to and stir them to mix nicely

11. Close up the lid and let it cook for 8 minutes at HIGH pressure

12. Quick release the pressure

13. Open it up and serve hot

Nutrition: Calories: 212 Fat: 14g Carbohydrates: 11g Protein: 12g

Recipes

Note:

26. Bacon Cheeseburger

Recipes

Preparation Time: 10 Minutes

Cooking Time: 30 Minutes

Servings: 4

Ingredients:

- 1 lb. lean ground beef
- 1/4 cup chopped yellow onion
- 1 clove garlic, minced
- 1 tbsp yellow mustard
- 1 tbsp Worcestershire sauce
- ½ Tsp. salt
- Cooking spray
- 4 ultra-thin slices of cheddar cheese, cut into six equal-sized rectangular pieces
- 3 pieces of turkey bacon, each cut into eight evenly sized rectangular pieces
- 24 dill pickle chips
- 4-6 green leaf lettuce leaves, torn into 24 small square-shaped pieces
- 12 cherry tomatoes, sliced in half

Directions:

1. Pre-heat oven to 400°F.
2. Combine the garlic, salt, onion, Worcestershire sauce, and beef in a medium-sized bowl, and mix well.

3. Form the mixture into 24 small meatballs.

4. Put meatballs onto a foil-lined baking sheet and cook for 12-15 minutes.

5. Leave the oven on.

6. Top every meatball with a piece of cheese, then go back to the oven until cheese melts for about 2 to 3 minutes.

7. Let the meatballs cool.

8. To assemble bites, on a toothpick, put a cheese-covered meatball, a piece of bacon, a piece of lettuce, pickle chip, and a tomato half.

Nutrition: Fat: 14g Cholesterol: 41mg Carbohydrates: 30g Protein: 15g

Recipes

Note:

Recipes

Note:

Recipes

Note:

www.ingramcontent.com/pod-product-compliance
Lightning Source LLC
LaVergne TN
LVHW010223190525
811635LV00008B/694